Dandelions Don't Bite

by Leone Adelson

Illustrated by Lou Myers

Pantheon Books

Acknowledgment is made to Harper & Row, Publishers, for permission to quote from *The Adventures of Tom Sawyer* by Mark Twain, to Dodd, Mead & Company for permission to quote the limerick from *The Complete Nonsense Book* by Edward Lear, and to Atheneum Publishers, Inc., for permission to quote the second stanza of "The Bridge" from *I Thought I Heard the City* by Lilian Moore, text copyright © 1969.

All rights reserved under International and Pan-American Copyright Conventions. Published in the United States by Pantheon Books, a division of Random House, Inc., and simultaneously in Canada by Random House of Canada Limited, Toronto.

Library of Congress Cataloging in Publication Data

Adelson, Leone, date . Dandelions don't bite.

SUMMARY: A brief discussion of the origins, spellings, and meanings of various words in the English language.

1. English language—Words—History—Juvenile literature. [1. English language—Words—History] I. Title.

PE1574.A33 422 74-39834

ISBN 0-394-92370-7 (lib. bdg.)

Manufactured in the United States of America

If you were a bee with a message to send
Or an ant that had something to say,
You might dance in your hive
In a kind of bee jive
Or wave your antenna or sway.

If a wolf you might howl, or hoot if an owl,
If you were a chicken you'd squawk,
But you needn't howl . . .

        . . . or growl

            . . . or yowl,

For you've thousands of words . . .

YOU CAN TALK!

To Lilian and her very special way with words.

Contents

How It All Began... Perhaps!

Who said the first word? What was it? How did it sound? *Nobody knows.*

There are no old phonograph records or sound films or videotapes to tell us. The beginnings of the spoken word are a mystery.

Language detectives, or linguists, have been hunting for clues to this mystery for hundreds of years. They have listened to the talk of people living in lonely places from the North Pole to the South Pole, from the deserts to the jungles, from the mountaintops to the wide plains. They have even studied the first sounds made by tiny babies. So far, there are no sure answers. But there are many good guesses.

If a baby says, *"pr-pr-pr"* as he blows bubbles with his cereal, is that a word? What is a word anyway?

All the printed marks on this page are words, of course. Who says so? Well, the dictionaries, for one thing. It's the job of the dictionary to tell us what we need to know about words.

Here is part of what my dictionary says about **word**:

1. something that is said
2. a speech sound or a series of sounds that has meaning.

Your own dictionary may tell you lots more.

4 Who else decides whether a word is a word or just a funny noise? *You* do! You . . . and you . . . and you . . . and all the you's in the world!

Whenever a great number of people decide that certain sounds would make a good, useful word, then those sounds become a new word.

Suppose all the people in your neighborhood decide to say, "Orningmoo Oodgoo" instead of "Good Morning." Then suppose other neighborhoods decide that they like the new greeting too, and soon thousands of people in the city and across the country are saying it.

"Orningmoo Oodgoo, Mrs. Jones."

"Orningmoo Oodgoo, Mrs. Smith."

Soon "Orningmoo Oodgoo" finds its way into newspapers, books, television, and radio. You may be sure that it will soon be found in the dictionaries too. A new expression has been adopted by the people.

Since the dictionary tells us that words are speech sounds, then perhaps the very first word was nothing but a sound someone made with his voice. It might even have been an accidental sound like the groan you make when you have hurt yourself. Or it might have been a strong puff of breath a tired cave man made when he came home from a hard day of hunting. *"Puh-pah-puh"* he panted, and it came to mean, "Whew! I'm tired."

The cave man made other sounds too—with his throat, tongue, teeth, lips, cheeks—when he was hungry, hurt, happy, angry. Soon everyone in all the caves around knew that these sounds, made the same way each time, always meant hungry, hurt, happy, angry.

Many linguists believe that language began just this way. They call it the Pooh-Pooh theory of speech because it may have begun with just the natural puffs of breath we make when breathing hard.

Other natural body sounds must have been added to this simple beginning—grunts, roars, sneezes, gulps, clicks of the tongue, whistles, or smacks of the lips. Indeed, there is an African language

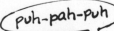
puh-pah-puh

Phew? Puh-poo-pah. Fah-foo...

Ha-hmff. Clck-clck...

Gluh-tch.

still spoken today in which clicks of the tongue are part of everyday speech.

If the Pooh-Poohers are right, a very early conversation in the history of mankind may have sounded something like this.

> Cave man: Phew! Puh-poo-pah. Fah-foo.
> (I'm tired. Is supper ready?)
> Cave woman: Ha-hmff. Clck-clck.
> (Right away, my dear.)
> Cave boy: Gluh-tch. T-t-t-oof. Mum-MUM.
> (Hurry it up. I'm starving.)

After all, do we not still hear people go, *"T-t-t-t"* and shake their heads sadly when they hear bad news?

A conversation between the cave man and his wife might have sounded just the way you sound when the dentist is working on your teeth and you suddenly think of something you *must* tell him right that minute.

But the Pooh-Pooh theory is just one guess. The Bow-Wow theory is another. According to the Bow-Wowers this is how language began.

A cave man came home from the hunt in great excitement. He had seen an animal he had never seen before. Getting down on all fours, he showed that it was a four-legged animal. He showed his teeth just as the animal had done when it snarled at him. He raised his arm to show the size of the animal.

His wife watched him, puzzled. Then he had a wonderful idea. In a deep voice he went, *"Wow-wow, bow-wow-wow,"* and from that time on Bow-Wow was the name of the animal because that was the sound it made.

In just the same way, *s-s-s-s* might have been the beginning of the word for snake, or *p-s-s-t* for an angry pussycat. Babies do exactly the same thing when they see a cow and go, *"Moo."*

The first men used all the sounds their bodies could make to form the first words. At the same time they probably used all these sounds to copy the sounds of their natural world as well as they could.

But these are only two of the ideas linguists have worked out in order to explain how the world's languages began. Isn't it exciting to think that from these beginnings, or something like them, have come almost four thousand different languages?

If you are reading this book, you speak the giant among languages—English. It is spoken by more people in more parts of the world than any other language. It has about a half-million different words. Where could they all have come from?

Let's see.

The Copycats

If you live near a large airport you may hear your father use some very special words when the passing planes rattle the dishes and wake the baby. Jet planes and rockets are still fairly new in mankind's history, although *you* cannot think of a time when there weren't any. Because they are so new, no one has yet invented just the right word to describe the sound jets make when they warm up or take off.

Not long after machine guns were invented someone coined the word "ack-ack" to describe the sound of the machine gun firing. When the new word for jet-engine noise does come along it will probably be another word like ack-ack. It will try to copy, or echo, in speech sounds how the jet sounds as it takes off.

Our language has many words that began as copycats of sounds. Dogs *yip*. Paper *rustles*. A stick breaks with a *crack*. Trucks *chug*. People *grumble*. Auto horns *honk*. You *cough* when you have a chest cold. Anything that makes a loud, sudden noise goes *bang*. Fat *sputters* in the frying pan. Clocks *tick*. Thunder *booms*. Water *splashes*. And do you remember the cereal that goes *snap-crackle-pop?*

 CAW

There would be no fun in hearing a lion roar if you could not tell your friends how frightening it sounded. It's easier (and safer) to use a word like "roar" than it would be to bring the lion home and let them hear it. So don't try it—say it!

In English we say that roosters crow with a *cock-a-doodle-doo*. But whether the rooster is crowing in Sweden or France or Italy or China he sounds exactly the same because he's neither Swedish nor French. He's just a rooster. But a Swedish child will say the rooster goes *ku-kukelik* (koō-kook-a-lik). A French child is sure that rooster goes *coquericot* (ko-ker-ee-ko). An Italian child says it's *chicchirichi* (ki-ki-ri-ki). And in far-off China the children say *kiau-kiau* (kee-ow, kee-ow).

It is plain to see that the people of those countries have tried to copy rooster talk with almost exactly the same sounds as we. But they use a different spelling for the same sounds. Most animal sounds are given the copycat words which people have invented.

BAA

 chirp

HISS

HOWL

It was a very long time ago when you surprised your parents by saying *"Ga-ga-ga."* On that great day your mother rushed to the phone to call your grandmother. "Guess what—baby's talking." You weren't really. You were playing with one of the many sounds in human speech—the *guh* sound you make in your throat.

You do many things with your throat—gulp, gag, gargle, gurgle, speak gruffly, gobble. All these words try to copy the sounds you make deep in your throat when you gulp or gag or gurgle or gargle. Even the throat itself is called a gullet. *Ga-ga-ga* was just a warming-up exercise for all these important words. So perhaps Mother was right and you *were* talking, though not yet in whole words.

Our speech machinery can make a great variety of sounds. When a new and different noise comes along (like the jet sound) we hunt through our storage warehouse of speech sounds to find just the right combination to say what our ears have heard—or what we *think* our ears have heard.

Pluck a guitar string. What does it sound like? *Twang* and *plunk* are pretty good copycat words for those sounds.

The wind blows through the trees with a *swish,* a *rustle,* a *stir.*

The same soft, breathy sound gives us soft, breathy words like *sigh, whisper, hush, kiss,* and *soft* itself.

A rusty door hinge or a shrill voice *creaks, squeaks, squeals,* and *screeches.*

The sound of things being broken or crushed gives us *smash, crash, squash,* and *crunch.*

Comic strips understand copycat language very well. They have invented a whole new bag of copycats—*Bam! Wham! Biff! Zowie! Pow! Oof! Zing! Zap!* and last but not least . . .

BOING-BOING

Have they become words or are they still just sounds? Look and see. Only one of these words is in my dictionary. What about yours? If enough people begin to use this comic-strip language sooner or later some of the words will be found in the dictionaries of the future.

You might say that they are standing on tiptoe saying, "Me too, me too!" as they ask to be let in as standard or proper English.

Cousins by the Dozens

In this picture people are trying to solve a puzzle. They are looking for the one right path through the maze that will take them to the center. There are so many turns and twists that some may never find the way. They may give up and go back, or they may keep on trying. Some get right to the heart of the maze with little trouble. Some get lost for hours!

Tracing words back to their beginnings is a little like following a maze. Sometimes you think you're on the right track only to find that it's going in the wrong direction. Back you go to make a new start, with another dictionary or word book to help you.

Take these three words for instance: **pancake, pansy, panic.** They look enough alike to fool you into believing that they may have the same great-grandparent word. But they are not in the same family at all, and never were. Their looks alone put you on the wrong track. *Pancake* is any thin cake baked in a flat pan over a fire. *Pansy* and *panic,* as we shall see later, have never met at all!

But with **mirror, admire,** and **miracle** it's a different story. These words are true Latin cousins, all of them coming from *mirari*—to look at or to wonder at with pleasure. Most people look at themselves in a *mirror* with pleasure—who does not *admire* himself! A *miracle* is something so strange as to be wondered at.

Finding word relatives is like discovering a cousin you never knew about before. "H'm," you say, surprised. "I must find out how she's related to me." Then you work your way back through all the family history of aunts and uncles and dozens of cousins and grandparents until you find the one great-grandparent you share with your new cousin. That makes you related to one another.

As you climb down your family tree in your cousin hunt, you may find Greek and Italian and Danish relatives sitting on the branches. One may have the family red hair but not the freckles. One may have great-uncle Jeff's big ears and curly hair, but not his long legs and wide shoulders. One may have the same dimple in the chin that your little sister has. But if you keep following the branches, you're bound to find the almost-forgotten relative who planted the family tree in the first place long ago.

The story behind a great many words in the English language is like this search. Many of the words that are closely related don't look alike or sound alike, nor are they spelled the same any more. They have changed greatly through the years, just as you will change as you grow older.

Look at **octopus, pedal,** and **pedestrian.**

Would you believe that the word for the great, slithery creature of the ocean—the *octopus,* or *octopod*—is a close cousin to the word for an important part of your bicycle—the *pedal?*

And both of them are related to the word for someone who walks along the road—the *pedestrian*. The ancient relatives of those words are an old couple—*-ped* (a Roman) and *-pous* (a Greek). Both these syllables mean foot. *-Ped* and *-pous* have had a great many grandchildren. *Pedigree, pedestal,* and *chiropodist* are some more of them. Can you see the family likeness in these words? If you're not sure, peep into your dictionary.

Pupil, puppy, and **puppet** have the same Latin ancestor, too—*pupilla,* a little doll or small person. A class of *pupils* are not just little dolls. But pupil has another meaning too, of course—the center of your eye. To find out what a little doll has to do with the pupil of your eye you must get someone to stand in front of you in a good light. Look deep into his eyes and what do you see? Yourself, of course! But how small you look! Like a little doll. Now that you know *pupilla,* it should not be hard for you to find out how *puppy* and *puppet* came to be related to pupil.

Here are some more word cousins and their stories.

clock, cloak   You must go way back to ancient France to trace these two English words. At that time, every village had a bell which could be heard everywhere. It rang every hour to give the time. This was a very important service because it was before alarm clocks or radio clocks or even cheap wind-up clocks that poor people could own. The French word for bell is *cloche.* When timepieces at last began to find their way into poor village homes, people still called them *cloches,* although they did not ring—they just ticked. When the word came into English, *cloche* became *clock.*

What could all this have to do with *cloak,* clock's cousin?

It's easy to see now that people wrapped in those long, warm capes looked like bells. But this time when *cloche* came into English, it made a slight change and became *cloak,* a bell-shaped cape.

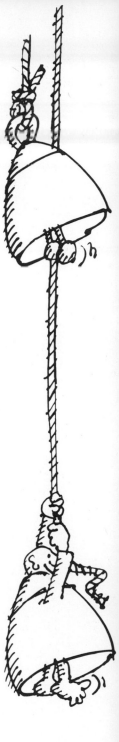

rival, river   When your school basketball team plays the team from another school, you might almost say that they are competing against a river. *Rival* and *river* grew from the same seed, a Latin one—*rivus.* But of course no river ever tossed a ball through a basket! People living on the banks of the same *rivus* were *rivalii,* or river neighbors, or *rivals.* Rivals depended upon their river for food, travel, and water for their animals. When the river ran low, each one tried to win more of the water for himself. Rivals came to mean those who compete against one another to win, not water, but games.

poodle, puddle   The root of both these words is an old German word—*pudeln*—that means splash, or wet. And there's nothing wetter than a *puddle* except a *poodle* dog that has been splashing around in a puddle. His love for the water gave him his name.

onion, union   Try to break an onion in half with your hands. It seems almost impossible. When you peel an onion, with tears running from your eyes, you can see how it got its name. The Latin word *unio* means "one." An *onion* is one tight *union* of layer after layer of vegetable matter. One must cut it to get it apart.

A tight union of people under one government is hard to break apart, too. "In union there is strength" may be said of both onions and nations.

pansy, pensive   All plants and animals have scientific Latin names as well as the names people have given them. These popular names are often made up by people who have a very lively imagination. Someone like that once looked at the pretty Viola flower and seemed to see a small face in its markings. It must have been a French person who took the French word *pensée*—a thought—and gave it to the little flower with the thoughtful face. It came into English as *pansy,* and also gave us another word for thoughtful—*pensive*.

paper, papyrus   We must leave Europe and go to Africa to understand this pair of word cousins. The Egyptians, who did not have beech trees in their hot climate, found another way to make pages to write upon. They used a water plant called *papyrus* to make a *paper* so strong that old papyrus scrolls are still found today, as good as when they were first written upon, thousands of years ago.

You are a cavalier from a cavalcade of cavalry and you have chivalry.

cavalry, chivalry, cavalcade, cavalier   The horse, or *cavallo,* is the connecting link that makes all these words related. The mounted horsemen of the old armies were the *cavalry.* Any armed horseman ready to fight for his king was a *cavalier.* A parade of cavaliers and cavalry was a *cavalcade.* In more modern times cavalcade became the word for a peacetime parade of horses or horse-drawn wagons. Today it is often used for parades without horses, too. In the days of knights a man's skill in managing his horse was very important. But just as important was his bravery, his honesty, and his courtesy. If he did not have these too, no matter how splendid his horsemanship was, he had no *chivalry* and was a poor kind of knight.

muscle, mouse   These two words, strange as it seems, have the same word ancestor far down on their family tree. It is the Latin word *mus,* or *mouse* in English. Another person with a lively imagination thought that the *muscles* of the arms of the Roman athletes of those days looked like little mice running up and down under the skin. Lucky for us that the English language separated *mus* into two different words or else today we might speak of muscle-traps to catch a mouse.

infant, infantry How soldiers (*infantry*) and babies (*infants*) could be related is hard to see unless you know that there is a Latin word, *infans,* which means "unable to speak." It is still hard to see how, unless you also know that a Roman law stated that all people under the age of eighteen were *infans,* or unable to speak for themselves in court. Now in those days, soldiers were taken into the army much younger than eighteen. They were all *infans,* and soon soldiers were called by that name. Our soldiers must be over eighteen, but the name has stuck, and *infantry* it became. Although not many of us ever become infantry, we have all begun life as infants.

book, beech If you were living in England about a thousand years ago and were spending a lazy summer afternoon reading under a beech tree, someone might say, "If you want Annie she's over there, reading a boc under a boc." *Boc* is Middle English for a beech tree. It has an inner bark which was used to make a kind of writing paper in those days, so a page of this paper got the name from the tree itself—*boc.* (We do the same thing today when we call the tumbler you drink from a *glass* just because it's made of glass.)

Pages of this *boc* paper, sewed together, became a *boc,* and in later English that word became *book.* Somehow, the *boc* tree made greater changes and became our *beech* tree. Anything can happen in a thousand years!

ball, bullet, ballot   When you came to these three words, you may have thought, "That's easy. I can figure those out for myself." You can make a pretty good guess, but you may have to check your dictionary for the whole story. This is about what you will find in most dictionaries.

> **ball**—a round or roundish body. [ME *bal*]
> (ME means Middle English. In the English spoken in England in the years 1100 to 1500, our modern word *ball* was written *bal.*)
>
> **bullet**—part of a cartridge for firing from small arms [t.F *boulet,* a little ball]
> (t.F means *taken from* the *French* word *boulet.*)
>
> **ballot**—1. a ticket for voting 2. (formerly) a little ball used in voting [t. IT *balla, ballota,* a ball or little ball]
> (t. IT means *taken from* the *Italian* words *balla* and *ballota.*)

So, if you thought that ball, bullet, and ballot all had something to do with ball, you were perfectly right!

This habit of borrowing words and bits of words from languages older than our own has not changed in modern times. That is one of the ways our language grows. Sometimes it seems as though we are even borrowing from ourselves! We used part of the word *cavalcade* (a parade of horses) to make *motorcade* (a parade of motor cars). We used it again in order to make *aquacade* (a program of water events).

However, since English is not a language that always follows its own rules, anyone who guessed that *lemonade* must be a parade of lemons would be making a mistake!

Where Did They Come From?

Some words tell their own stories. One look at *spring* and *fall,* a second to think, and we know the reason why these names were given to two of our seasons. New plants spring up in the spring; leaves fall in the fall of the year. It's very clear why the *swing* in the playground was given its name. There can't be any mystery about what time of the day the *sunrise* comes.

But other words are harder to understand and they have to be coaxed to tell us about themselves and where they come from.

Most of us have worn *jeans* at one time or another. If we thought about it at all we might have supposed that it had something to do with the name of a girl. Not at all. The truth is that it comes from the name of the cloth from which jeans are made. This strong cloth was first made in Genoa, Italy, for sailors' pants that had rough wear. It was known as Genoese cloth and began to be used for overalls and work pants. Genoese became *Genes* cloth, and then *jeans* cloth. The name was finally given to the pants themselves.

foxglove Kittens never wore mittens, nor did foxes ever wear gloves. The blossom of this plant looks so much like the finger of a glove that it might have "foxed," or fooled people.

duck A duck paddles smoothly across a pond. Suddenly, down goes his head beneath the water and up comes his tail instead. He gets his name from this habit of dipping, or *duck*ing his head under the water to get at something good to eat.

handkerchief This word started out as kerchief—to cover (*ker*, from the French *couvrir*) the head (*chef,* or *chief*). When it was tied around the neck to keep off drafts it naturally became neckerchief. As houses became less drafty neckerchiefs were just carried in the hand as pretty ornaments. Now that we have a special kerchief for the head and a special one for nose-blowing perhaps the name will be changed again. What about *handkernose*—carried in the hand to cover the nose? *Nosekerchief?* Only time will tell.

pocketbook What we call a wallet today was the original pocketbook of two hundred years ago. A pocketbook then was a small folding case, like a small *book,* carried in a man's *pocket* to hold paper money and important papers. But after ladies began carrying them too, and stuffing them full of all the things ladies carry, pocketbooks grew larger and larger until they outgrew men's pockets. So men took to carrying small billfolds in their pockets and let the ladies carry the pocketbooks over their arms.

kidnap is made up of two slang words—*kid* (young child) and *nab,* or *nap* (to grab, or steal). Strangely enough, although they have always been slang words, they came together to make a proper English word. It was coined long ago when young boys and girls were being stolen away from their homes to work in America. Kidnap still means stealing people away, but usually for money rather than for work.

dandelion The name of this little yellow, shaggy flower that grows like a weed, did not settle down to its present spelling until it had been back and forth between France and England several times, centuries ago. From the sharp, jagged edges of its leaves it got the name "Lion's tooth." When the French invaded England, many English words took on French accents. The little lion's tooth plant became the *dent-de-lion* (tooth-of-the-lion). Then it took on an English accent and became *dandelion*. As you can see, *dent* means tooth. Does that give you a clue to some other words, having to do with teeth, that have *dent* in them?

mushroom is made up of two words that have absolutely nothing to do with this delicious vegetable, or fungus. *Mushroom* is what the English long ago thought the French were calling it. What they were really saying in their own language was *mousseron.*

curfew today means "everybody indoors and off the streets." It is actually two old French words—*couvre* (cover) and *feu* (fire). In the old days a village warning-bell was rung each night. At the sound everyone had to go indoors to cover their cooking fires with ashes so that the houses would not catch fire during the night and burn the village. Without light or heat there was nothing to do in those days but go to bed. Today most children's camps and all army camps have a *curfew* or "lights out" time. In troubled times a city government may order a curfew—a time when citizens must be indoors.

bulldozer   The history of this word is quite different from its present use. Today bulldozers are the powerful earth-moving machines used in building or road-making. But at one time a bulldozer was a man with a very special job. With a noisy crack of his bull whip (bullwack), he helped to move great herds of cattle across the plains. This was called "giving them a dose of the bull" by the *"bull-doser,"* or bulldozer. A good bulldozer could move cattle safely, without losing or stampeding them. Because he was such a powerful mover, the same name was given to the great machines that can move mountains of earth and rock.

school   Can you imagine your mother telling you that you might not go to school until you had straightened up your room, taken out the rubbish, gone to the store, and babysat with your sister? In other words, until you had the free time in which to enjoy yourself? That is exactly what *scholē* meant in ancient Greece—free time. When people had *scholē* they learned and studied, so *scholē* took on a new meaning—studying time, and became our *school*.

butterfly   Yellow butterflies seem to be more common than other kinds. Butter is yellow, so these pretty insects became known as the "yellow-fliers," or "butterfliers." Now, whatever their color, they are our butterflies.

caterpillars have been on this earth for as long as there have been insects. In every land they had a name in the language of that land. Our own word for these fuzzy creatures comes right from the old French name *catepelose*. It really means cat-hairy from *cate* (old French for cat) and *pelose* (hairy). If it sounds better to us as hairy-cat, it should rightly be pillarcater. Caterpillar or pillarcater, neither one has anything to do with cats. Some words have led puzzling lives.

You can begin to see what a great mixture our language is. It's like a huge, rich, delicious stew with all kinds of words in it. There it is, a big pot full of English all stirred up and bubbling away. From time to time a word in the stew may cook away and disappear. But then along comes someone with a new idea and a new word to throw into the stew to make it richer.

You can be sure of one thing. As long as there are people to keep the pot going, the word-stew will continue to bubble away, getting better all the time.

New Words From Old Ones

"Whole be thou."

Next time your phone rings try answering it with these words. It is more than likely that the person calling you will say, "Oops! Wrong number. Sorry." And yet, all you said was, "Hello." Since this is the twentieth century, you would not dream of saying, "Whole be thou!" or even, "Hale be thou!" But they are the great-great-great-grandfathers of today's hello.

Like Cinderella who lost her slipper at the ball, these early greetings have lost some of their letters (and their sounds, too) in their hurry to get into modern English. It is certainly true that you wish your friends to be well and healthy (whole and hale), but time has worn down these expressions to a shadow of their former selves—a modern, streamlined hello.

Because this greeting goes back so very, very far in man's history, its beginnings are buried in Old and Middle English, French, German, and Scandinavian. Just to make its history even harder to trace, there are a few early printers' spelling mistakes thrown in too. So it is not surprising that not all linguists agree that our modern hello was once "whole be thou." Some believe that hello came from *hallo,* which came from *hollo,* which came from *hola.* Many languages are behind our poor hello, who by now must be wondering where indeed he came from.

Hola, it's this way!

Hale be thou! No it's this way.

And what is *hola?* Why, it's what you shouted to the ferryman when you wanted him to come back across the river and row you to the other side. After a while it became merely a greeting which you used whenever you met a fellow traveler on the road.

Sometimes a new word gets its foot in the door, like a good salesman trying to sell a vacuum cleaner, and remains to make a sale. Sometimes it is pushed out again. "Sorry, we don't need one." No sale.

Hello made the sale, although it lost some of its parts on the way. There are many words in our language which tried many forms of themselves—usually longer ones—before settling down to the words we now use. Here are some of them.

The day's eye's my favorite flower

This word	was once this
daisy	*the day's eye* When its white petals opened to show the yellow center, it was like the sun looking down on a new day.
o'clock	*of the clock* "Five of the clock and all's well." The apostrophe (') warns us that something is missing, as in won't, can't.
alone	*all one* "There is no one with him—he is all one."
because	*by cause of* "He died by cause of a fever."
piano	*pianoforte* A foot pedal added to the old-fashioned harpsichord made a new

It's 5 of the clock ...I'm all one by cause of mother's out...

instrument of it. And a new word, too. Now the music could be made soft or loud, *piano* or *forte* in the language of the Italian inventor.

bus   *omnibus*

This Latin word means "for all," and was borrowed by the French as the name of a new kind of large coach or carriage, cheap enough "for all" to use. People in a hurry soon shortened it to *bus,* and bus it has remained, even after the horses went out and the motors went in.

After I practice pianoforte I will take the omnibus to Jack's house.

nickname   *an eke name*

At one time people had only a first name. But there are only just so many first names. Soon it became confusing to say "John" with six Johns in the same village, so people began *eke*-ing, or adding, last names. *Eke* name, said carelessly, became *nekename,* and then *nickname.* Today a nickname is an extra first name your friends (or your enemies) tack on to you, like Shorty, Red, Fatty, or Lefty.

My eke name is Fatso but I'm not really fat...

taxi,
or cab   *cabriolet*

Cab was shortened from *cabriolet.* This light, one-horse carriage was not like the heavy coaches of the day. It could leap through traffic like a *capra,* or goat. Cab became

It's these pantaloons.

taximeter cab when the meters were added for the tax, or fare, for each ride. Then it was shortened to taxicab and finally it became just taxi, or cab. If taxis leap like goats, so do the poor pedestrians who have to jump out of their way.

pants *pantaloons*

A comical actor of fifteenth century Italy invented a kind of costume to wear on the stage to make people laugh even more. He never wore anything else, like our own Charlie Chaplin and his big shoes. People began calling his costume after him—Mr. Pantalone and his pantaloons. They even began wearing pantaloons, too. So do we, but we call them pants and we have changed their style—but styles change faster than words. What will the pants of the Space Age look like?

farewell *fare ye well*

In the days of bandits, wild animals, bad roads, broken coach wheels, and wash-outs on the road, travel was a serious business. The family's blessing, "Fare ye well!" was more than just a polite hope that the traveler would fare, or get along, well on the road.

Fare ye well!

goodbye *God be with ye!*
. . . and fare ye well!

Here To Stay

Imagine this conversation taking place at your home some Sunday evening.

> Mother: I'm too tired to cook this evening.
> Father: Why don't you rest while the children and I get together a nice old-fashioned Sunday night supper? Come along, children, we'll run down to the *delicatessen* and get some *macaroni* and *potato* salad with *mayonnaise*—
> Son: —and *frankfurters!*
> Father: A can of *goulash* with *dumplings*—
> Daughter: —and *pizza!*
> Mother: Will you get me a little *salami?*
> Father: It sounds like a regular *smorgasbord.* Come on, kids.

And so you put together a very good meal. But it is not an "old-fashioned American" meal because in the early days of our country such foods could be found only in the countries they came from—Italy, France, Germany, Hungary, Sweden. However, it did not take long for them to get here. They came, names and all (sometimes spelled a little differently), right along with the immigrants.

Almost all of us can trace our family beginnings back to another country. Large cities like New York, Chicago, San Francisco, Milwaukee, and Boston have neighborhoods of Polish, Irish, Mexican, Italian, Armenian, German, Swedish and Arabian people, or their children, grandchildren or great-grandchildren.

Think about your own ancestors. Where did they come from? When the people came so did their customs—their food, language, holiday celebrations, and all their ways of living.

Who does not like to eat! Everyone does. That is why so many of the foreign words in the English language seem to be for good things to eat. Many of the wonderful mouth-watering foods from Italy alone can make a delicious dinner. (If you're hungry you had better skip this part.)

First, the *antipasto*—what you eat before (*anti-*) the main meal (*pasto*) to give you a good appetite—*pizza,* and spicy sausages like *salami, bologna,* and *pepperoni.* Now the soup—*minestrone,* "the big soup," thick with beans and vegetables. Next comes the *pasta.* Pasta is nothing but a paste made of flour, eggs and water, but to the Italians and now to us it is our *spaghetti, macaroni,* and *ravioli.* If you have room for dessert, have some Italian ice cream—*spumoni* or *tortoni.*

French cooking is known the world over, and many French

dishes are now part of American cooking: *soupe,* which we spell without the *e, mayonnaise, omelette, fricassee, tartes* (tarts), *toste* (toast), *bonbons.* The French cook who makes all these good things is the *chef,* the chief or head cook of the kitchen.

The Germans and the Dutch gave us *hamburgers* and *frankfurters,* from the German cities of Hamburg and Frankfurt. Our German and Dutch settlers brought us *sauerkraut* too, as well as *dumplings, cookies, crullers, pretzels, pumpernickel, seltzer, cole slaw, cranberries,* and last but not least—*noodles* and *strudels.*

Our close neighbors, the Spanish-speaking people of Mexico, have given us hot *tamales, chile con carne, tapioca, vanilla, bananas,* the *barbecue* way of cooking, and the *cafeteria.* The word *barbecue* is only slightly changed from the Spanish *barbacoa,* which means a little raised platform on which you build a fire to roast your meat. In *cafeteria,* the Spanish-French word for coffee (*café*) is plain to see. Once just a small shop for coffee and other drinks, Americans have made it a restaurant where you choose what you want and carry it to the table.

Spanish was the first European language of our southwest, just as cattle-raising was the first business of the southwest. Many of the Spanish words of the horse and cattle business are still with us. The movies and television have helped to make it so. Doesn't this sound like a program you have seen?

> The cowboy puts on his *sombrero,* saddles his *pinto* pony and rides off through the *canyon* to the *rodeo.* He wins the bucking *bronco* contest and gets first prize—a beautiful *palomino* pony. The horse and the cowboy parade around the *corral* while everyone cheers. But a sudden rainstorm chases everyone home, so our cowboy puts on his *poncho,* and riding his new *palomino,* sets off for his *rancho.*

But long before the settlers from Europe came, bringing their languages with them, there were three hundred Indian languages being spoken by the Indians of North and South America. Many of their words have become ours. We can thank the Aztec Indians for the words for two favorite foods—*chocolatl* and *tomatl*. It didn't take long for chocolate and tomato to make their way around the world!

But the most important food of the first settlers was the Indian *rockahominy,* or dried corn. They called it hominy, and it is doubtful if they could have lived through those first hard winters without it. They even learned the Shawnee Indian way of cooking it, first grinding it, then mixing it into a paste and baking it over an open fire to make "Shawnee cakes." Shawnee cakes sounds like Johnny cakes, and Johnny cakes they became, to fill many a stomach when our country was younger and poorer than it is today. Another use of Indian corn was in *m'squitquash* which, even today as succotash, is a boiled mixture of corn and beans.

Ashatsquash became our squash, *pawhicorra* nuts are today's hickory nuts, and our pecan nuts came from the Indian *paccan* tree. Explorers, travelers, and woodsmen of those early days before roads, motels, and restaurants learned another Indian custom which saved many lives in the days of discovery. From dried meat and fat, with sometimes a few dried berries added, they made *pemmican,* a hard meatcake, easy to carry but hard to chew.

The Indian words were difficult to learn and there were no printed books to learn them from, so the settlers wrote them down as they thought they heard them. If you had never seen the word *thought,* do you think you could have spelled it right just from hearing it?

So it is not surprising that *seganku* is our skunk, *arrakun* is raccoon, *moos* is moose, *pasiminim* is the persimmon fruit, the soft deerskin slipper of the Indian, his *mokhisson,* is the mocassin we still wear, and *chitmunk* is our little chipmunk friend.

Countries as far away as Australia have added words to the English language. We have kept the native words for kangaroo (*kanga* means "jump") and boomerang, the curious throwing stick of Australian bushmen which comes right back to them when they throw it.

If anyone asks you if you speak any other languages beside English, you may honestly say "Yes, many!" All these words, used all the time, are foreign ones, with some slight changes in spelling. *Kimono*—a Japanese housecoat. *Algebra*—a form of arithmetic first used in Arabia. *Bamboo* and *ketchup*—a plant and a sauce from the Indonesian islands. *So long!*—in Malay this form of goodbye is *salang. Chimpanzee*—a word in the Congo language of Africa.

If you live in a *bungalow,* so do many people in India, where

...shawnee cakes, succotash and ashatsquash, pemmican with pawhicorra nuts, rockahominy with tomatl...

I like chocolatl

How about a bath? You smell like the seganku.

a little house like this got its name. Those pretty cotton materials, *calico* and *chintz,* were first made in India, too. And if you are ever in Borneo and need to talk about a "man of the woods," just say *orang-utan,* for that is what they call their huge, man-like ape. And so do we.

English is a language that usually finds the shortest way to say something. After the "horseless carriage" was invented it was given a better name: automobile. That was soon shortened to auto. Now almost everyone calls it a car. What could be shorter than that!

Not all languages are always in such a hurry to get something said. The American Indians made up words for things which described how they looked or acted, or how they felt about them. The word *arrakun* (raccoon) means "he who scratches," and *moos* (moose) means "he who strips" (bark off trees). The great Mississippi is the "father of waters." The German word *delicatessen* means "delicacies (good things) to eat." In America we are beginning to shorten that to "deli." The German people would never recognize their word! This custom of naming things by describing them has given us many interesting words.

Pajamas (or pyjamas) is made up of two words from Persia, where pajamas were worn in the street by both men and women. The Persian words mean "clothing for the legs." Once baggy and full and worn by day, they are now straight and slim in Western style, and are for nighttime wear.

Chauffeur and **garage** are French words. Now they are our words, too. In French, to heat something up is *chauffer.* Since the earliest automobiles ran by steam engines instead of batteries, they had to get up a good head of steam in order to go. It was the *chauffeur,* "he who heated up," who got the engine going so he could drive away from the *garage. Garer* means "to protect," and a garage is a protected place for a car.

Kindergarten is another German word. It really means "a garden of children," but it is hard to understand why that name has stuck. When you were in kindergarten did you remain planted in one place for very long?

When the first astronauts made their victory visits to American cities, they were almost buried under showers of tiny bits of colored paper which we call confetti. In Italy, *confetti* are little colored candies. If it meant the same thing in America, there would be little work for the streetcleaners to do after the victory parade!

A dragon, to us, is a great fire-breathing serpent met only in myths and fairy tales. The ancient Greeks called it *drakon,* which describes the creature perfectly. It means the "quick-glancing terrible eye" monster.

The English language is beginning to pay back for some of the words we have borrowed. The word-traffic across the oceans is now becoming a two-way street instead of a one-way street. That is because foreign countries are using some of our words, as we have used theirs. They may not spell them quite the same way, or even say them as we do, but it's easy to recognize them just the same.

The Russians take fotografs...
and drive automobils...

Can you recognize *futbol* and *beisbol?* The whole world plays them! Many Japanese use *hankechis* to wipe their noses, *pen* and *inki* to write letters, and a *naifu* and *foku* to cut their food and eat their dinners.

The Russians take *fotografs,* drive *avtomobils,* pay their bills by *chek,* and go to the *gospital* when they are sick.

If you like to sleep outdoors you can find *campings* signs all over Europe. If you like hot dogs, that's what they're called in Europe too! So are sandwiches.

The first blues, jazz, and rock music was played in America and the sound soon spread clear around the world. Even if it's called *buki-wuki,* we know that it's going to sound like our boogie-woogie.

So if you travel abroad and if you speak only English, don't be afraid—you will not be nearly as much of a stranger as you might think!

...and go to the gospital

Patchwords

These and many other "almost" words are knocking at the door of standard English. They may go on knocking many years before they are invited to come in and sit down. In the end, they may be turned away because they have been forgotten. Or they may go out of style. Or people may find better words for the same thing.

While they are waiting to be made standard English the dictionaries themselves may not be sure, because not everyone will be using them. So, many dictionaries do let them in—for a while anyway. Usually such words are marked "slang," or "colloquial" or "regional." This means, "we know some people use them, but we're not sure where they came from and we're not sure if they are going to stay, SO USE THEM AT YOUR OWN RISK!"

Words like *absotively* and *slanguage* were made up when someone tried to find just one right word for what he wanted to say. Not finding it, he put parts of two words together to make a new one.

In the same way, ladies make new bed covers from bits of old clothing and curtains and sheets. New covers made from stitching old pieces together are called *patch-quilts.* We might call our put-together new words *patchwords.*

You are using a patchword when you order a cheeseburger at the lunch counter.

Cheese sandwich + hamburger = cheeseburger

You are using a patchword when you say, "Let's stop at that motel."

motor car + hotel = motel

Just imagine a time when people may travel about in their own planes or helicopters or even with their own set of wings as they do in their cars today! They might not want to land each night at a crowded airport to sleep at a motel or hotel. Floating skyports may be invented where they can spend the night in a new kind of floating hotel with a new patchword name.

For guests of motels and skytels who oversleep and get up too late for *breakfast* but too early for *lunch* a patchword has been coined to take care of that in-between meal—*brunch.*

In a zoo one day a strange kind of cub was born with a *tiger* and a *lion* for its parents. What to call it was a puzzler until someone thought of naming it after both parents—a *tiglon.*

When you *twist* something around and *whirl* it in the air at the same time, as the Majorettes do with their batons when they lead a parade, this motion is called—*twirl.*

A sound that is something like a loud *clap* and something like a *crash* gave us—*clash.*

When a *flame* bursts upward, lighting up everything around it with a bright *glare,* we have—*flare.*

A candle flame that *gleams* softly begins to *shimmer,* or shake, if a breeze blows on it. A gleaming, shimmering light is a—*glimmer.*

Sad to say, modern cities often have clouds of either *smoke* and *fog,* or *smoke* and *haze,* hanging over them. Two patchwords coined for these conditions are—*smog* and *smaze.*

Since smog and smaze often tickle the nose, it may not be long before still another patchword is coined to take care of that special kind of nose-tickle—smog and smaze make people *smeeze!*

Sometimes two entire words, instead of just parts of them, are put together to make a new word. Catbird, skyscraper, workman, rooftop, sunshine, moonlight, playground, and many, many more like them are quite easy to understand. There are others which join together and make quite a new meaning. It is just like mixing together two different colors to make a brand new one. Red and blue paint mixed together give us purple; yellow and blue give us green.

Toadstool is such a word. It is neither a toad nor a stool but a kind of mushroom. In long-ago days when folks believed in fairies and elves and other magic creatures of the woodland, perhaps someone truly believed that toads sat upon mushrooms when they became tired of hopping about!

Cowboy is the same kind of patchword. If you put a cow and a boy together it would seem that a *cowboy* should look like this, but we all know what a cowboy really looks like.

Patchwords like these can be very confusing to a foreign student who is learning English. How can he know that *shorthand* has nothing to do with the length of one's fingers! When you write shorthand you use lines and curves instead of letters. How can he know that nobody blows a *shoehorn!* Shoehorns are for slipping tight shoes on easily. They were made from the horns of cattle.

What do you suppose our student thinks the first time he hears the word *pigpen?* Like horn, *pen* has more than one meaning. In this case it means to fence something in.

Do the police go fishing with a *dragnet?* Not at all. Putting out a police dragnet means that all the police stations in the city have been warned to search for certain law-breakers before they get away.

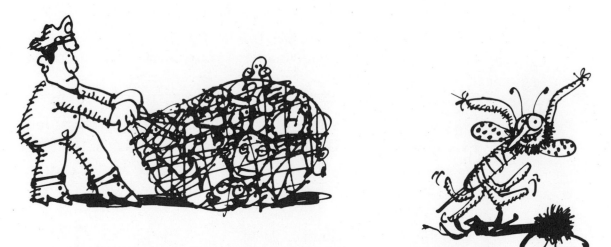

And whatever would he think about *jitterbug?* It certainly sounds more like a nervous insect jittering or wiggling about than a dance, although you do have to wiggle about when you jitterbug. By now he might have caught on to some of the tricks the English language plays, and he might figure out for himself that a *litterbug* is just a very untidy person.

Patchwords are the shortcuts in the language. Instead of saying that someone is "stubborn as a pig," we say he is *pigheaded.* When you play Pin-the-tail-on-the-donkey, it would take too long to say, "Let's fold a handkerchief and put it around his eyes so he can't see." The patchword *blindfold* is much simpler. It's easier to say "What's for *breakfast?*" than "What's for the first meal in the morning?" The idea behind that patchword is that you have slept all night without eating and you break your fast with the morning meal.

Lewis Carroll, who wrote *Alice in Wonderland,* was very fond of inventing patchwords. His most famous one was a bit of a *chuckle* and a bit of a *snort* put together to make *chortle.* A chortle is a kind of laugh made partly in the throat and partly in the nose.

"'O frabjous day! Callooh! Callay!' he chortled in his joy." The poem *Jabberwocky,* in which this line appears, has so many patchwords in it that Lewis Carroll had to explain them. But even without understanding what he meant exactly, we somehow get a creepy, crawly feeling right from the opening words of *Jabberwocky:*

'Twas brillig and the slithy toves
Did gyre and gimble in the wabe:
All mimsy were the borogoves,
And the mome raths outgrabe.

People must have needed a word like chortle, for it has become a standard English word. But all the rest of the *Jabberwocky* patch-words have remained right where they were—in Mr. Carroll's book, still making people chortle.

Far Away And Long Ago

The ancient Greek people had many gods and goddesses whom they made the master spirits of their natural world. Everything had its own special god to whom people prayed—sun, air, water, fire, plants, animals, and even love.

The little god of flocks and forest creatures was a cheery, friendly god, but unhappily for him he was a very ugly one. Added to his hairy body he had the horns, feet, and tail of a goat. His looks were so wild and startling that when he came near people they ran away in fright. All he wanted was to dance and play sweet music upon his reed pipes, but all he did was frighten people half to death for no good reason.

The little god's name was *Pan.* The word we took from it is *panic.* We have another, longer word—*pandemonium*—that also describes what happens when panic breaks out and people lose their heads for little reason. (In today's slang, when you say to a friend, "You know, you're a panic" you can see how far you are from the word's true meaning.)

The story of Pan is only one of the hundreds of myths, or stories, which the ancient Greeks, Romans, and Scandinavians made up about their gods. Perhaps there was some magic about them after all, for many of them are still alive in our language.

ocean

Oceanus was the father god of all the ocean nymphs and of *Ocean,* the great endless river which the Greeks believed circled round and round the flat earth. To go from one side of the earth to the other, one merely set sail upon *Ocean.*

echo

A beautiful nymph named *Echo* was punished for chattering too much. She lost all her power to say what she wished. All she could do was to repeat the last few words of whatever she heard people say. She could not even tell handsome Narcissus that she loved him, so she crept unhappily into a cave where her sad voice is still heard, only able to *echo* what she hears you say.

siren

The *Sirens,* who lived on a rock in the sea, caused many shipwrecks. Their siren song was so loud and clear and sweet that sailors drove their ships upon the sharp rocks so they could get a good look at the singers. Instead of being warned by sirens, as we are today, the ancient sirens made sailors lose their ships and their lives, for none of them ever came back.

cereal

The beautiful, beloved daughter of *Ceres,* goddess of fruits and *cereal* grains, was kidnapped one day. She was forced to spend half of each year in the Underworld of the god Pluto. Ceres was heartbroken. She decided to punish the world. From then on, fruits and cereals were allowed to grow only during the seven months of each year that her daughter was returned to her.

tantalize

Tantalus was a god so cruel and mean that he was sent to the Underworld for an unusual punishment. Though cool water and fresh fruits were all around him, he was tied to a tree and could not reach them. He could not eat or drink or die, and so was *tantalized* by hunger and thirst forever.

mercury

Mercury was the gods' messenger. With wings on his feet and on his hat, carrying his magic wand, he ran so fast he hardly touched the ground. The fluid metal in a thermometer (also called quicksilver) which rises and falls with the temperature is called *mercury* because of its rapid movements.

furious

There was much mischief and wrong-doing among the gods as well as among the humans. The three horrible *Furies* were in charge of punishing all such wrong-doers. With snakes for hair, the faces of dogs, and the wings of bats, the Furies never rested in their *furious* search. Who would not be furious if he looked like the Furies!

atlas

Zeus, the chief god, wanted to punish *Atlas*, who had fought against him in a war. He decided to rest the entire earth and the sky above it on the back and shoulders of Atlas, to hold forever. From the name of this mighty god comes the word for a book of maps of the world—an *atlas*. From the same god comes the name of our great ocean—the Atlantic.

volcano

Even gods needed iron tools, wheels, and weapons. *Volcanus* was the blacksmith of the gods, hammering away beside his fiery furnace, which roared as he worked. In those days it was believed that when a new *volcano* burst forth on earth, it was because Volcanus was working beneath that mountain.

January

Janus had two faces, so he was able to look both ways at once—a handy thing for the god of doorways. He was also known to the Romans as the god of good beginnings. For good luck, they named the first month of the new year Januarius. The first month of the new year became *January* for us, too. (A doorkeeper was once known as the janitor.)

The Romans named their third month after *Mars,* the great god of war. *March* is our third month, too. It does not seem to be more warlike than any other month, unless one thinks of spring and winter fighting it out between them during that windy month. Many words connected with military things come from the same god of war—Mars: the *marching* of soldiers, the foot-tapping music of a *march,* the word *martial* itself, which means military. One of our largest planets was named after Mars. People like to play with the idea that there might be life on that planet and they have already named its imaginary beings *Martians.*

It was the Greeks and Romans who began to name the planets that rule the sky after the gods and goddesses who ruled *them.* Our scientists continue to do the same thing as each new heavenly body is discovered. A chart of the solar system looks like a roll call of Greek and Roman gods.

The Greek god of the underworld and of darkness was *Pluto.* A dark new planet discovered in 1930 gave off so little light that Pluto seemed like a very good name for it. The ancient Greek god was thought of again when scientists made a new radioactive material for atomic bombs and chose to name it *plutonium.*

When our space scientists looked for names for the rockets, satellites, and other space wonders of the twentieth century, they chose names like Zeus, Apollo, Jupiter, and Mercury. The Greeks of two thousand years ago would look with wonder on what is happening to their gods today.

The ancient Scandinavian people had their gods, too. They named the days of the week after them. We have kept many of those names. Their chief god, who made the earth, was *Wodan.* His special day, Wodan's Day, is now our Wednesday. Wodan's mother, *Frigga,* the goddess of love, gave us Frigga's Day—Friday.

His son, *Thor,* the thunder god, named our Thursday, and *Tyr,* the god of the athletes, was honored on Tyr's Day—our Tuesday.

So far we have been dealing with imaginary beings who lent us their names. There have been real people, too, who have named everyday things for us.

The English Earl of the Sandwich Islands is with us in our lunchboxes most days of the week. The Earl of Sandwich was a great card player. He hated to leave the card table, even to eat. One day he solved his problem. He slapped a big slice of meat between two chunks of bread and kept right on playing—and eating. These days we put everything from mashed potatoes to bananas between bread but we still call them *sandwiches.*

No one today would dream of drinking milk that had not been *pasteurized* first. And yet, until a French scientist, Pasteur, invented a way of treating milk to make it safe to drink, no one worried about raw milk fresh from the cow.

Flowers like *zinnia, dahlia,* and our Christmas flower, *poinsettia* were named after the scientists who first grew them.

When a group of people decides not to trade at a certain store until the storekeeper changes his way of doing business, that is a *boycott.* An Englishman, Captain Boycott, managed a large farm in Ireland, but he was so unfair to the workers on the farm that they would no longer work for him. They would not buy any of his milk or eggs or vegetables and soon he stood quite alone in the village with no one to give him a hand. It must have worked, for Captain Boycott soon gave up and went back to England, leaving his name behind him.

If you're lucky enough to have a warm, waterproof *macintosh* for wet, cold winter days, thank the inventor *Charles Macintosh.*

It was his idea to add India rubber to the cloth used to make this type of raincoat.

Many other words we use were named after their inventors. You can find these in your dictionary: zeppelin, cardigan, guy, saxophone, doily, guillotine, bloomers.

When your grandfather was young, he probably went to school wearing *knickerbockers*—knickers, for short. They look very funny to us today, but boys never wore long pants until they were young men. Golfers wore them, too, at a time when ladies wore bloomers for hiking or biking. Knickers got their name from the Knickerbockers, a nickname for the early Dutch settlers of New Amsterdam, who wore such pants. Both knickers and bloomers have gone out of fashion, but old styles have a habit of coming back, and when these do we'll have names all ready for them.

When a linguist starts out on a word hunt he never knows where he will end—it may be in history or science or fashion or cooking or medicine or art. Paths from all these and many more lead right up to our great English word bank. So help yourself to words—they're free!

The Language Beanstalk

this way to the year 2000

UNABRIDGED DICTIONARY

½ million now

150,000 year 1700

60,000 year 1500

40,000 words year 1000

What giant steps this giant English language of ours has taken during the last thousand years!

The drawing shows the numbers of words linguists believe were in the dictionaries of those years.

The famous beanstalk that Jack planted did stop growing at last, but the English language beanstalk shows no signs of stopping. It has grown and grown until only a strong man can lift a complete, or unabridged, dictionary of today. Will it ever come to an end? The answer to that is probably, "No, never." Things that are alive never stop growing or changing.

Not that language is alive in the same way that plants and animals are alive. You cannot take language home for a pet, or water it and watch it grow, or remind it to take an umbrella when it rains. Then is it really "alive?"

My dictionary says first that alive means "full of life." Perhaps that definition is not very helpful all by itself. So we read on in our dictionary: "Full of action, power, energy." Just to make sure that we have truly covered the ground, we look up the word "life." We find that it grows from a very ancient root, spelled in several ways—*leip-*, *loup-*, *lip-*. It means "to continue, to last." Certainly language is full of action and power. It has the power to gladden us or to sadden us or to madden us. It has the power to make us proud or ashamed or afraid. It has the power to move us to action or to feel something deeply.

You feel a certain way when you hear the words loving, gentle, friendly, snug, cozy. But you feel a very different way when you hear earthquake, accident, fright, ghost, nightmare, explosion!

The words of Columbus moved King Ferdinand and Queen Isabella to give him the ships and the men he needed for his great voyage. Patrick Henry's "Give me liberty or give me death" helped to move the American colonies to break away from England. Martin Luther King's "I have a dream" moved people all over America to share his fight for civil rights for all.

Certainly language is continuing, or lasting, although it is not entirely the same language it was a thousand years or five hundred years ago. Many words have changed their forms. Old words die off as people stop using them. They become "obsolete." We no longer say, "When the bull chased me I *clomb* a tree." These days we say *climbed*. Nor do we say, "My neighbors *holp* me to cut the hay in the *mead* before the storm." *Helped* and *meadow* have taken the place of those obsolete forms.

Some words die off when they're no longer needed. That almost happened to *pillion*. It was a very useful word in the days when horses were used for travel, and two people rode on the same horse. The second one sat behind on the *pillion* seat. The word all but disappeared when modern transportation came along, but it has come to life again with the motorcycle's pillion seats for the second rider.

As with many living things, growth may sometimes take on a new and unexpected shape. A branch of a tree may suddenly shoot out from the trunk where no branch grew before, and change the shape of the tree. Or a wart might suddenly begin to grow on the end of someone's nose and give the nose a funny shape it never had before.

Such changes happen to words, too. Some of them grow new meanings and become strangers to their old selves, just as though a brand new word had been added to the language.

Silly is one of those words. Once upon a time all it meant was cheerful, happy, good. It had the same sense and sound as its German cousin *selig* (blessed). A bride and groom were *silly* because they were blessed by good fortune. Then the meaning of the word changed to mean weak or timid; "silly sheep" were so called because they were afraid of their own woolly shadows. Today silly means foolish or stupid.

Naughty once meant poor. Poor people were naughty people—people who had *naught* or nothing. Since they had naught of any value this was a bad thing, and so naughty began to mean bad or worthless. Today a child who does not obey or is full of mischief is naughty. Our arithmetic word nought—a zero—is really the same word, spelled differently.

Nice is a word that has gone through more changes than almost any other. If you had told someone he was "a nice boy" a few hundred years ago you would have hurt his feelings. Nice comes from the Latin word *nescius,* which means not-knowing, stupid, so to tell someone he was "nice" would have been an insult. From stupid it came to mean wild and willful, then it meant shy, then foolish, then hard-to-please, then for a long time it meant careful and exact. Today nice is just an overworked word for something that is pleasant. No one knows for sure why some words change their minds.

Our language is like a room with many doors. Through one door come all the words borrowed from foreign languages, like *igloo.* Through another door come the words that are really their inventors' names, like *saxophone,* invented by Adolph Sax. Another door lets in such words as *telescope,* which we make up from old Latin and Greek roots as we need them. Another door opens to let in the copycats, like *squeak,* and the patchwords, like *flunk.* All their stories are told in your dictionary.

Still another door is well worth watching, for the in-and-out traffic here is very great. This is a door we might mark colloquial (used more in conversation than in books) or slang. For them the word-room is like a waiting room. Will they be admitted into the dictionaries or not? That depends on how popular or useful

they are, or how long they last. If they do last (like joy-ride or jukebox) the dictionary-makers will mark them *"colloq."* or *"slang."*

Most slang words seem to be invented by people with lively imaginations who are tired of using the same old words for the same things or who have coined a new word for a new thing—like *jive,* for swing music.

Styles in slang change very fast. Early in this century it was *hip* (today's slang for *smart*) to say *skiddoo* when you wanted someone to get out or to go away. Today it is a very old-fashioned slang word. Many new ones meaning the same thing have come and gone: skedaddle, scram, beat it, get lost, take a powder, and the newest—split. By the time you read this split may be out and skiddoo back in!

A friend is not only a friend but a chum, a pal, buddy, pardner, or sidekick.

There are all these ways of saying head—noodle, noddle, bean, block, dome, nut, cocoanut, wig, knob, button, cabbage, attic, bonnet, conk.

As for money, you may also say: bees and honey, mazuma, spondulix, dough, moola, sugar, cabbage, lettuce, shekels, bread.

Something false or not quite right can be: fake, phoney, baloney, applesauce, bunk, horsefeathers, banana oil.

A different kind of word-coining is used for names of the new

exciting inventions of modern times. For these we generally dig among the Greek and Latin roots of our language in search of bits and pieces that have the meaning we need. So, when a marvelous underwater ship came along we chose the Latin *sub–* (under) and *mare* (sea) to make the perfect name for a *submarine.* The Greek *tele–* (far-off) added to *phone–* (sound, voice) gave us *telephone,* which brings voices from far away. At first the wonderful motor car was called a horseless carriage, but something so special had to have a special name. From *auto–* (self) and *mobilis* (movable), came the name for that self-moving new wonder, the *automobile*—no horses needed!

Man loves to tinker—he tinkers with things, and with words to fit the things. What great new idea is perhaps this very minute being born in the mind of a tinkerer? Perhaps it is a kind of powerful receiver that will be able to bring back from outer space sound waves which may have been floating there for hundreds of years!

Just imagine turning a dial to a wavelength marked "Nineteenth Century." Click-click. Suddenly we hear the voice of Abraham Lincoln: "Fourscore and seven years ago our fathers brought forth upon this continent a new nation . . ."

If that dream should ever become real let us have a name ready for it. It must have something to do with *phono–*, or voice, of course. We dig among the Latin roots again. Here is one that means backward—*retro*. That's it! *Retrophone*—the machine that brings back vanished sounds. We have created a new word for a new idea.

Creators of new and beautiful things are the artists of the world. There are artists who work in paint and in stone and in wood and in music. There are artists who work in words. With words they create pictures for our mind's eye as other artists do for our body's eyes and ears. How can we ever forget how Huckleberry Finn looked after we read in Mark Twain's *The Adventures of Tom Sawyer*—

> His hat was a vast ruin with a wide crescent lopped out of its brim; his coat . . . hung nearly to his heels and had the rearward buttons far down the back; but one suspender supported his trousers; the seat of the trousers bagged low and contained nothing; the fringed legs dragged in the dirt when not rolled up.

Words take us by the hand and lead us right into the once-upon-a-time world, as in the beginning of the famous English Fairy Tale "The Well of the World's End"—

> Once upon a time, and a very good time it was, though it wasn't in my time, nor in your time, nor anyone else's time, there was a girl whose mother had died, and her father married again. And her stepmother hated her because she was more beautiful than herself . . . At last, one day, the stepmother thought to get rid of her . . .

With words that have the swing of music, a great unknown writer of the Bible tells about the coming of spring:

> . . . for lo, the winter is past, the rain is over and gone. The flowers appear on the earth, the time of singing has come, and the voice of the turtledove is heard in our land . . .

And there are words—such as Edward Lear's—that tickle our
funny bones—

A was once an apple-pie,
   Pidy,
   Widy,
   Tidy,
   Pidy,
   Nice insidy,
   Apple-pie!

You can do anything you like with the right words. No one
knows this better than poets. With their special way of seeing
and their special way of feeling. Lilian Moore wrote of the city—

A bridge
at night
is spun of light
that someone tossed
across the bay
and someone caught
and pinned down tight—
till day.

For century after century after century a great treasure of words
has been building up. Most treasures are locked up and put away
for safekeeping. But not language! The more that treasure is used
the longer it lasts. Whenever you use a word, you help to keep
it alive. Words that are not used disappear from our language,
and new ones come along to take their places.

A poet has said, "Language is made by the people." And it's
what people say that counts!